Corporate Sisterhood
The Ultimate Power Prescription
for Every Working Woman

By Dr. Jacque Colbert, D.M., M.S.M., C.P.C.

Published by Jacque Colbert
www.jacquecolbert.com

First printing September 2016

Paperback ISBN: 978-0-9981021-0-8

E-book ISBN: 978-0-9981021-1-5

Printed in the United States of America.

This book is dedicated to my parents,
Roy and Noreen Walters.

Just like moons and like suns,
With the certainty of tides,
Just like hopes springing high,
Still I'll rise.

—Maya Angelou, "And Still I Rise"

Introduction

When I was in high school, I went to work on Wall Street. No, I wasn't an investment prodigy, but I *was* a nerd and a bookworm—and my parents had instilled the pursuit of excellence in me. I was determined to rise to the top in all endeavors. That's how, in the fall of 1986, I found myself on a subway train bound for lower Manhattan instead of walking my usual route to Samuel J. Tilden High School in East Flatbush, Brooklyn. I had been accepted to a cooperative education program, alternating between a classroom full of kids and an office full of bankers at Irving Trust, whose headquarters were located at One Wall Street.

The main building is one of those Art Deco wonders, somehow constructed during the Great Depression, with a banking area that looked like a cathedral. Irving Trust added a less impressive annex in the 1960s; however, I was assigned to work in the beautiful skyscraper. It was a completely different environment from anything I had experienced, and that was the point. The idea behind the program was that I would learn about the business world and start paving a path to a career in Corporate America. I did eventually rise through the ranks of that world, but what I really learned at Irving Trust was this: in an organization where most of the power brokers are men, the women who stick together, rise together. And if those women can reach across differences (in everything from ancestry to their taste in music), they will rise even farther.

The woman who planted this idea in my head (an idea I would later see proven in published research) had a desk right across the room from me. On the surface, we had nothing in common. Her name was Rosemary, and she was much older than I was. She was also Italian

American. I'm African American, but when I say that, I'm referring to *both* Americas. I was born in South America, in the former British colony of Guyana, where my parents had lived for over three decades. My father was a foreman doing construction work and back in those times, my mother was a dynamic homemaker, effectively managing the nuances of running a home and taking care of eight children. We were fairly poor back then although I didn't know it. My dear grandmother, who will be 94 years old this year, was already in the United States in the late '70s, and it was she who sponsored our entire family to come to the Unites States. We immigrated to New York City in the early '80s when I was still a shy teenager.

Rosemary and I had backgrounds that were literally worlds apart, but she took me under her wing, showed me the ropes, and did her best to sing along to my ever-present Reggae music. That was thirty years ago, when I had an unmistakable Guyanese speech style that faded as I grew older. Rosemary would belt out the lyrics to various reggae songs thinking she had nailed my dialect, but what she was producing was actually a lot closer to Jamaican/American Creole. It didn't matter that she didn't get it right, and that she wasn't in tune with the subtle details of my birthplace. I was drawn to her open, friendly, expressive, hilarious personality; she was truly like my sister from another mister—and from another culture. Having her on my side helped me grow on a daily basis. Rosemary taught me a lot, including how to haggle for the best prices for the things that I wanted. One of the best examples of the way she helped me occurred when I learned the difference between American baseball, basketball, and football. All I knew was cricket and soccer, but I quickly became a Mets fan.

The sisterhood skills I started learning with Rosemary would take me all the way to top leadership positions at one of the world's largest technology firms, and then at a top firm in the petroleum industry. But not right away, because by the time I walked across the stage to receive my high school diploma, I had decided that the walls of a company like Irving Trust were not big enough to contain my dreams. As far as I was concerned, I had already proven myself in the Big Apple. Plus, I hated the bitterly cold New York winters. I wanted to see the world, and be all that I could be, so, much to my parents' anguish, I decided to postpone college and join the United States Army. That was the first significant turning point in my life: defying the wishes of the people I had loved dearly all my life. They were convinced that nothing good would come out of my military service, and I was convinced that I would prove them wrong. I made a promise to myself to not only rise through the ranks, but to do it fast.

I was determined to soar to the highest heights in every task that every drill sergeant put before me. With every scream in my ear and every push-up that I pushed out of my then-leaner body, I was determined to go far. When my four-plus years of service concluded, I had been promoted three times, immersed myself in the culture of my South Korean posting, and learned leadership instructions from some of the finest minds I've ever encountered. My parents associated military service with people who aren't very smart (yes, a bias based on a negative stereotype), but I showed them that you have to bring your mental A-Game—not just physical strength—when you're serving and protecting. By the time I returned to civilian life, concluding my service at the rank of Specialist-E-4, I had made my parents proud, thanks to the Army sisterhood, which is in a class by itself, filled with remarkable women.

Whether you are at the very beginning of your career, full of dreams mixed with trepidation about your future, or you have been in the workplace for a decade but feel like you just can't get ahead, or you have made it to the C-Suite and want to make sure your team becomes the very best that it can be, this book will teach you how to reach in, reach out, and ultimately reach for the stars by joining forces with your Corporate Sisters. Back when I was a teenager, a network was built in person, on handwritten or typed Rolodex cards. Today, technology makes it possible for you to connect with like-minded Corporate Sisters around the globe, and to stay connected to sister-colleagues long after you're not at the same organization anymore. If I could have flash-forwarded to the future, I would have asked Rosemary to connect with me on LinkedIn and perhaps even asked her to give me a public recommendation. But Corporate Sisterhood is about much more than building an impressive online profile. It's a state of mind that calls you to actively seek ways in which you can give others a hand up, and to actively seek those women who share your vision and can cheer you on while you rise to your full potential (and, more importantly, set you straight when naysayers question your ability). This book showcases not only my personal tried-and-true strategies for moving ahead, but it also incorporates my findings from a research study I conducted in 2011 and 2012.

The research was born out of my father's continual urging that I take my education to the limit. What he meant by this was the *pièce de résistance:* the doctoral degree. By the time I was 28, I had delighted him by returning to the original, pre-Army plan, completing a bachelor's degree and a master's degree (with a concentration in HR) at Baker University. I was sprinting up the ladder, moving from managing a tech-industry call center (which at one point had 700 seats) to joining the company's key strategists on all aspects of talent management, talent acquisition, organizational change, and other crucial elements of the company. "Yes, but how about that doctorate?" Dad asked. My dad could be relentless about my education because his love for me was relentless.

In 2008, I thrilled him by being accepted to a doctorate in management program, but soon after my classes began, my "organizational change" skills were put to the test. A routine mammogram led to a biopsy, which led to a terrifying doctor's appointment during which I received a diagnosis that I did not want to believe at first: breast cancer, stage 1A, requiring a lumpectomy, radiation, and chemotherapy. This is a sisterhood nobody wants to join, but in this case, sisterhood was a matter of survival to me. I was otherwise in top physical condition: why was this happening to me? And why now, just when I was about to embark on the toughest mental challenge of my life? Part of my physical strength came from the fact that I teach boot camp classes. In fact, I taught one of those classes on the morning of my surgery. My wise father, Roy Walters, was looking down from heaven watching me beat cancer; he did not live to see me complete my doctorate. Nevertheless, his confidence in me has proven to be everlasting, and it shaped chapter six of this book, which is dedicated to the fact that becoming a strong woman doesn't mean sequestering yourself from strong men who want to help you become a champion. In that chapter, I pay tribute to the progressive men who saw my potential, and I offer advice for fathers who want to be the kind of dad Roy was, always striving to help their daughters make the most of their talents and reap the rewards accordingly. I was equally blessed to have a "*Shero*" in the form of my wonderful mother, the quietly persistent, unflappable Noreen Walters.

With her in mind, while my medical team and I were conquering the tumor, I chose the topic for my dissertation research. I was inspired by a ground-breaking study conducted in 2006 by Catalyst, a nonprofit research and advisory organization whose stated mission is to work with businesses "to build inclusive environments and expand opportunities for women at work." The study that was of greatest interest to me was titled "Connections that Count: The Informal Networks of Women of Color in the United States." Catalyst's many conclusions included the observation that African American women at work tend to follow a "sticking together" approach instead of a "blending in" approach; in other words, they are unlikely try to develop connections with their white counterparts, particularly their white male counterparts (who hold most of the positions of power in corporate America). So it's no surprise that African American women participating in the study tend to have a high percentage of same-race affiliates within their networks.

What are the effects of this phenomenon? The Catalyst researchers found that advancement rates for African American women to executive levels were positively associated to the number of other African American women within their networks, indicating that they're using the sticking together approach very effectively. But I wanted to know more. How do we reconcile that finding with the fact that so few top executives are Black women? The situation hasn't improved in the years after I concluded my research. In 2015, only four Fortune 500 CEOs were Black, and only one of those four—Ursula Burns, Chairman and CEO of Xerox—is a woman. As I set out to understand and explore the phenomenon, I invited sixteen women to participate in a one-on-one interview with me. I focused on women in the information technology sector in order to provide a common denominator in terms of the industry. The women were all African American and had earned at least a bachelor's degree, and all of them had held a senior leadership position for at least ten years. In those recorded interview sessions, I gathered data on themes, benefits, and challenges that they had experienced in breaking through the glass ceiling, and the role Corporate Sisterhood played in helping them thrive despite those challenges.

I'll tell you all about my findings in chapter three, but what I gleaned personally from that project—while continuing to heal physically from my illness, without taking a leave of absence from work—was that Corporate Sisterhood not only sustains women in the workplace, but it sustains the corporation itself. The word "corporation" is derived from the Latin word for "body." Just as my body activated its "all hands on deck" network of healing, corporations benefit from internal networks that rally to support one another.

Corporate Sisterhood is not about gossip at Happy Hour (though women's friendships at work are sometimes perceived that way, as frivolous or even a drain on productivity). Corporate Sisterhood is in fact a corporate asset. It's about helping each other rise, and as the internal teams rise, so does the organization as a whole.

How many more women could rise to the C-Suite, or Congress, or the United Nations, if we all tapped the power of Corporate Sisterhood? Though the participants in my study were African American, many of their experiences will resonate with women workers of all ancestries, and the inspiration for these chapters comes from far-reaching sources. My research subjects offered strategies for success that are universally eye-opening. At the same time, some of their perspectives are unique to the experience of women of color. This book will give you the inspiration and the preparation to achieve two levels of sticking together—joining hands with the broader network of women in your profession, and also joining hands with a mini-network of truly kindred spirits who, like my research participants, share a unique place in history.

The audience for this book includes my precious daughter. I call her my little blackbird: Raven. I was once told that when one becomes a learned person, one never sees the world the same way again. I have lived through many turning points and witnessed many transformations in America, but after the birth of my daughter in 1993, I finally became a learned person. That's because becoming a mother opened my eyes to the joy of selflessness. As the eldest daughter of eight children (six boys, two girls, me being the third in ranks), I dutifully and lovingly cared for my siblings. Yet I know firsthand that becoming a parent, through any means, can open your heart in a special, new way. When I looked at my daughter's tiny, trusting face for the first time, I saw hope, and the ability to do the impossible! So she is part of my motivation. By inspiring others, I hope to build an even more joyful world in which she, and all the daughters in her generation, can uncover their calling, focus on their purpose, and rise to levels of achievement that are far higher than any Manhattan skyscraper.

Fending for yourself is a fool's errand, but I have seen a rising tide of self-serving, winner-takes-all leadership gaining popularity. With *Corporate Sisterhood*, I hope to turn that tide. If we stick together, the supply can be infinite. The supply is only scarce if an organization stops thriving (a surefire outcome if an organization stops functioning as a unit). No matter where you are on the ladder of life, it is my hope and my prayer that these chapters will empower you to join the exquisite company of women just like you, who strengthen and sustain each other every day, in every corner of the globe. That's where the heart of success truly resides. Now let's start rising!

Your Corporate Sister,

Dr. Jacque

One

A Report from the Front Lines, from the Break Room to the Board Room

Making Things Happen

"When you get women in roles of leadership, we make things happen." This widely circulated quote was uttered by Melinda Gates when she addressed a gathering of female leaders in Berlin in 2015. German Chancellor Angela Merkel had invited power brokers ranging from the director of the World Health Organization (Margaret Chan) to the president of Liberia (Nobel Prize winner Ellen Johnson Sirleaf). As someone who entered the workforce when most of the world's power brokers were men, I get a thrill thinking about Merkel's summit of women who had truly reached the summit. The quote appeared in a *Forbes* article on the summit published that same year, written by Carolyn Howard, and Melinda Gates made it to the cover of the magazine (seeing a woman on the cover of *Forbes* is still thrilling to me, too).

But what Gates went on to say underscores what women around the world know all too well. As the highly competent co-chair of the Bill and Melinda Gates Foundation (the wealthiest private foundation in history), she followed up her visionary statement with a practical statement about how we make it a reality: "It takes us using our voice, and it also takes us making investments, huge investments, in women and girls." With a science degree as well as an M.B.A., Gates is known for championing an analytical approach to philanthropy, supporting what is proven to work and testing outcomes with a high level of precision. But I think it takes a woman to fully appreciate the rewards of investing in other women; she was giving voice to the sway of sisterhood.

I started this chapter with that lesson in current events because it's an often- overlooked part of our strategy sessions. Let's think of our GPS for a moment. What are the two things your GPS needs to know before it can calculate your route? Obvious answer, you're thinking: "It needs to know my destination, and my current location." While you're reading this, you're surely able to picture your destination. You have this book in your hands because you want a career in which you're paid what you're worth, your work is fulfilling, and you have a voice in shaping the way that work is accomplished. But how much do you really know about your current location? This chapter is designed to help you take stock of your situation and, like Melinda Gates, learn how to invest your resources wisely for maximum payoff. But when you start achieving those payoffs (or if you already are), you'll reap the reward of true satisfaction if you can follow Gates's advice and reinvest your part of your payoff in helping other women and their daughters rise alongside you. It's like a compounded rate of return: the dividends of Corporate Sisterhood should be earning dividends themselves.

So where are we now? What is the status of women in corporate America in the twenty-first century? Let's start by looking at statistics from Catalyst, which, as I mentioned in the introduction, is a nonprofit research and advisory organization whose stated mission is to work with businesses "to build inclusive environments and expand opportunities for women at work." Visit their Knowledge Center online at www.catalyst.org, and you'll see that as of July 26, 2016, women in S&P 500 companies:

- Comprise 44.3 percent of total employees (that's an upward trajectory I contributed to starting in the 1980s, when women certainly didn't comprise almost half of the S&P 500 workforce)
- Comprise 4.4 percent of the CEOs

That's right; you're not seeing double. We make up about 44 percent of the total S&P 500 workforce but hold only 4.4 percent of the top positions. Does this mean that most women in those organizations are in low-level positions? Actually, no. The following numbers should give you hope. Women in S&P 500 companies:

- Comprise 25.1 percent of executive/senior-level officials and managers
- Comprise 36.4 percent of first/mid-level officials and managers

What's hopeful about that? I can hear you hollering at me, "Jacque, how can you be hopeful if women are in the minority in those leadership roles too?" The answer is that these roles are the gateway to moving ahead. If those managers can mentor the women who work for them (and we know those women are there, because they represent nearly half of the S&P 500 workforce!), the Corporate Sisterhood effect can start delivering that compounded interest.

The numbers do form a daunting pyramid (Catalyst titled the whole report "Pyramid") because the presence of women tapers off as the levels of power increase. This book is designed to help us invert that pyramid. The numbers show that the gate is open (far more open than it was for our mothers, and for their mothers).

I have literally seen the changing face of the break room and the board room. Back in the days when people actually took an hour away from their desk for lunch, the break room was generally populated by women eating sandwiches they'd brought from home (and later, microwave meals with microscopically small portions). It was a sign of the pay scale. The people who could afford to go out to lunch, or who were given expense accounts for all-important client meetings, or who were decision makers who got to be wined and dined by vendors? Most of the people in that category were guys. Today, men and women alike are usually hunched over their keyboards throughout the lunch hour, but my point is that the break room's lunchtime population of low-wage, entry-level workers *has* evolved. The population of the board room has evolved too, but on an infinitesimally small scale. Breaking out of the break room was one small but important step for womankind. We have the momentum to rise, and when we do rise to those positions of power (remember how I started this chapter?) we make things happen. Say it with me: WE MAKE THINGS HAPPEN.

That's much more than just a clever slogan. It's backed up by copious research. Take your pick. How about the findings of a study co-written by the Peterson Institute for International Economics and EY (Ernst & Young), released in 2016, which showed that promoting women to the highest corporate office correlates with increased profitability? Think the findings might be skewed by small sample size? Not for this study. Peterson and EY looked at nearly 22,000 publicly traded companies, located in 91 nations around the globe.

How about Catalyst's landmark 2007 study, "The Bottom Line: Corporate Performance and Women's Representation on Boards," which examined return on equity, return on sales, and return on invested capital at Fortune 500 companies? In Catalyst's follow-up article, "Companies with More Women Board Directors Experience Higher Financial Performance," researchers examining this empirical data found that "companies with the highest representation of women board directors attained significantly higher financial performance, on average, than those with the lowest representation of women board directors . . . [and] notably stronger-than-average performance at companies with three or more women board directors."

How about the findings of a 2015 study published by the McKinsey Global Institute, titled "The Power of Parity: How Advancing Women's Equality Can Add $12 Trillion to Global Growth"? Envisioning the results of the Melinda Gates approach, the researchers found that if every country narrowed the gender gap "at the same historical rate as the fastest-improving country in its regional peer group, the world could add $12 trillion to annual gross domestic product by 2015."

I'm sharing these data with you for several reasons. First, it gives you evidence for any naysayers who, out loud or through their body language, have let you know that they think women are "too soft" to get results when they're playing in the big leagues. (A seemingly progressive male executive told a friend of mine that when he was on a recent flight, the pilot was a woman, and this made him nervous: would she have the physical strength to maneuver such a big plane if something went wrong, and the mental strength to come up with a logical solution?)

The second reason I'm giving you these statistics is that I want to inspire you. If, deep down, you still question yourself and wonder if those naysayers are right and you really are "too soft" to get real results, we can reverse that brainwashing once and for all. The Corporate Sisterhood can and does deliver results: it's time for us to reinvest those results in creating even greater opportunities for each other, moving on up from management to top leadership. We're good for business!

There's a third reason I'm supplying you with these statistics is to help you form a new habit. Statistics provide a much-needed reality check, and they've never been so easily available online. It's harder to bamboozle a population when they have a high-speed Internet connection and the know-how to access free (and freeing) facts about their place in the world. Get in the habit of "standing in your truth" (as Suze Orman calls it) by regularly looking up the facts from trusted sources—not conspiracy theorists on Facebook. This chapter will end with an exercise to help you start forming that habit, and the truth you discover will not only set you free, it will help you rise.

You cannot reach your destination if you don't even know where you are.

Next Steps: Dr. Jacque's Human Resource Inventory

I love the term "human resources." When I was starting out in the business world, that department was usually just called Personnel, like a storage facility where all the "persons" were waiting to be plugged into the corporate machine. "Human resources" puts the emphasis on our humanity—we're human beings with unique talents and temperaments—and it emphasizes the fact that we're all resources, with something of value to offer the organization.

These days, you really are your own Human Resources Director. Many corporate recruiters rely on online networks to find the best candidates, giving you unprecedented access to opportunities and the people who are managing those opportunities. Answer the following questions every year (even if you're unemployed: in fact, ESPECIALLY if you're unemployed; you can simply write N/A beside the questions that don't have an answer at the moment). Use this annual checkup to adapt your game plan while staying the course.

Ideally, you will answer every question in every category, even if it takes some research, but if that's too overwhelming, at least make sure you don't skip a category.

PART ONE: YOU

1. What are your talents? Make a complete inventory. Think back to when you were in school, noting the classroom assignments that came easily to you and brought you joy, the achievements you feel proudest of (on and off the job), and the activities for which you routinely receive the most praise. If you've received negative performance reviews, ignore what wasn't working. This inventory is about determining what is working; that's a good signpost for determining your purpose.

2. Where are you on the career ladder right now? What is your job title now? How much are you earning? What is the dollar value of your benefits, if you're lucky enough to have benefits (health insurance premiums, retirement contributions, paid time off, etc.)? If you were to become seriously ill (as I did, when breast cancer reared its hideous head), how much would you have to pay in medical expenses before you reached your out-of-pocket maximum on your health insurance policy? These are the kinds of

questions that help you look beyond the simple salary, calculating your true compensation package.

PART TWO: YOUR ORGANIZATION

1. Is your organization growing or declining? Where does your company rank with competing firms? What are the brand traits and/or mission statement/values of your organization? Are those in line with your personal goals and values? Where you work, what skills are the most in demand, and what skills are a dime a dozen? Are you overqualified for your job? If so, what's keeping you from applying for a more challenging position? What new skills can your firm help you gain, through training and/or mentoring? What are the responsibilities and expectations of your boss's boss? Where did your boss's boss go to school? What is his or her management style? Is it working?

2. What are the criteria for promotion and raises at your organization? What are the required qualifications (including certifications, degrees, and software knowledge) for the current higher-paying job openings at your company? If your firm recently experienced a reduction in force, what made the difference between those who were laid off and those who got to keep their jobs?

PART THREE: YOUR PROFESSION

1. Consult with Glassdoor or another online tool that provides salary information. What is the typical salary for your current position, in your part of the country? What is the next rung on your career ladder, and how much do those positions typically pay? Use LinkedIn to examine job openings for positions in your field,

and keep track of how many candidates applied (this isn't available for all LinkedIn postings, but you'll often see it). Which postings seem to get a deluge of applications? Which postings seem harder to fill?

2. Consult with the Bureau of Labor Statistics online. Is your chosen profession growing or declining? Are there new, emerging fields for which your skills would translate well? What opportunities do you see for you to participate in a new wave of innovation?

PART FOUR: YOUR WORLD

1. How big is your world of work? And is it big enough to accommodate your personal vision for your life? By this, I mean how far (geographically) does your professional life take you? Are all of your co-workers in the same town as you, or does your employer have a worldwide network? As a high school student, I had already lived in two countries and was eager to travel even farther. Maybe you love your hometown and want to remain there with your family. Maybe you want to move to a bigger city. Maybe you want to move to a small town and work remotely. However your world is defined, what skills and traits are valued there? How are you expanding your network to grow and thrive? Are there any cultural differences that you could learn about to help you flourish even more in that world? What are you doing to make your world a better place for your Corporate Sisters?

2. How is the global economy affecting your work? If your job has been offshored, what are the working conditions and wages for the person who is now doing your job? What aspects of your work could never be offshored? What are you doing to help your Corporate Sisters on the other side of the globe, the sisters you will never

meet and who perhaps have neither voice nor visibility? Corporate Sisterhood must extend beyond the walls of corporations. Keep Melinda Gates's mandate at the forefront of your thinking: What will it take for us to see more women into leadership roles? "It takes us using our voice, and it also takes us making investments, huge investments, in women and girls."

After you have finished this inventory, you'll have a well-stocked warehouse of information. Draw on it to show your team, your supervisors, and particularly your Corporate Sisters how you are adding value to the organization and to the world around you. Use it to formulate and communicate your aspirations, moving to higher ground if you see a storm on the horizon.

Portrait of Power: My Army Sisters

As I mentioned in the Introduction, I took a detour between high school and college. That detour was called the United States Army, and it led me first to Fort Jackson, in South Carolina, for Basic Training, followed by Fort Sam Houston in Texas for Medical/Urology Technology specialty training. I was later stationed in Seoul, South Korea, where I enjoyed the best of times. But the most important place the Army led me to was my own self. I discovered what I thought my physical and mental limitations were and then surpassed all expectations. There's nothing like a drill sergeant to help you find out what you're made of. It was the ideal starting point for my journey, and I wouldn't trade the experience for any other. Most of all, I was forced to work with others as a unit, joining a sisterhood whether I wanted to or not. The process of self-discovery and world-discovery I'm prescribing in this chapter is much easier to accomplish with feedback, wisdom, and facts from your Corporate Sisters.

My first Army sister was named *Reid*, from Saginaw, Michigan. She was my bunk buddy, and I just called her Reid because there's no place for first names in Basic Training. Reid and I shared a tent on many occasions before we went our separate ways to permanent duty stations, but we helped each other "stand in the truth" during those first weeks by watching each other's backs during our allotted time for guard duty, when we were mandated to be on watch during the night—never leaving our post until properly relieved by another soldier. We were also each other's biggest supporter on those long road marches—I'm talking *long*, as in 15 miles with a 50+pound rucksack and an M16 A1 rifle.

For the remainder of my time in the Army, I was blessed to share the bonds of sisterhood with many other strong young women, particularly Shawn (Margo) Cash, Desiree Dawn Seaton, and Terri Potts Carmona, whom I met when I was reassigned to South Korea. Our sisterhood was special because inasmuch as each woman was different, each one taught me something different and vice versa. Shawn was the youngest of the bunch, and she brought vitality and vigor to the group. She would dare us to do things with her easy-edgy Atlanta style and we'd fall in line—you couldn't help but love her yet be an exemplary big sister. On the other hand, Desiree and I bonded out of our South American/Caribbean affinity. She brought wisdom and character beyond our ages and at that time, we needed it. In my mind, she represented the voice of reason. We all loved each other very much because that's what you have when you're thousands of miles away from home in a strange land.

If Ramen noodles were all we had, we shared it and made the best of it. Being in Korea was daunting when we first arrived, but through our quick bonding and sticking together, we made the very best of what could have been a very long year away from the familiar grounds of the United States. During our time in Korea, we found ourselves either watching TV together, shopping, going out to the Enlisted Club or just encouraging each other. We had each other's back and in true sisterhood style, we took cover for the other when needed, opened up a shoulder for someone to cry on, whether the situation related to being away from home or simply trying to figure out the ups and downs of life as a young woman in a male-populated Army. To this day, Terri and I are such close friends that no matter how much time has passed since our last visit, we can pick up a conversation exactly where we left off.

I want to close by mentioning Ann Smith because she taught me something I truly needed for my journey in life. She taught me how to drive—yes, Ann taught me how to drive. When I entered the military, I was a true New Yorker. I knew how to pitch my subway token into the slot, but I didn't even know how to start a car. I was so scared in Ann's little bright orange Datsun that my entire body would shake. Then again, she was probably a bit more scared given the way in which I jerked the steering wheel from side to side when attempting to drive. For the sake of safety, Ann and I would drive around the neighborhood, primarily in our cul-de-sac area. My depth and distance perception were so off; I was drenched in sweat with each lesson.

Through all of our lessons, I have to believe that while Ann was teaching me how to drive, I was teaching her patience for when her first-born arrived; I was named godmother to her son, La Brandon. Ann was also the best garage-sale shopper I have ever met (and believe me, knowing how to find and separate the jewels from the junk at a garage sale is a skill). She was from Jackson, Mississippi, and when I attended her wedding there my world expanded even more.

She eventually was reassigned to Alaska, but I thank her for teaching me that teaching itself—especially teaching a skill that requires overcoming a fear—is one of the greatest gifts of sisterhood.

Dr. Jacque's Power Prescription #1

Become your own Human Resources Director, continually researching the facts about your individual job market, your marketability, and broader shifts that affect your livelihood.

Personal Reflections

Given what you've just read in this chapter, and taking the key elements of the power prescription, use this page to reflect on and write down things that you're doing and will continue to do, as well as things that you should be doing differently as your own Human Resources Director.

Two

A Brief History of Laboring Women

Women's Work in America

I know what you're thinking: "I want to move forward! Why is Dr. Jacque making me look back? The history of working women is painfully fraught with harassment and exploitation." My dear Corporate Sister, I'm not asking you re-hash what you already know. I'm asking you to stand on the shoulders of a long line of survivors and thrivers. I'm asking you to build on the momentum set in motion by thousands of girls and women around the world who triumphed— decades, centuries, or even millennia ago. Their history is your history, and their milestones will remind you that by moving ahead in your career, you too are making history.

"Toil" has always been part of the human experience as men and women alike sought to keep themselves fed, sheltered, and defended against predators. Childbearing obviously had an impact on the division of labor between men and women, but the most significant aspect of that division is what the Bureau of Labor Statistics calls "labor force participation," referring to paid labor in the workforce. Once humanity began owning land and selling goods, the balance of power naturally shifted to those (almost always men) who pocketed the payoff. Women have always been toiling, but without being able to participate in the world of work beyond the home, that toil went unpaid. Until the Industrial Revolution, which required droves of paid workers (even if they were egregiously underpaid), very few women had the ability to build wealth. The New Testament mentions an early convert to Christianity named Lydia, and she is described as a woman of financial means who dealt in the textile trade (with access to costly purple dye), but ancient references to women like Lydia are few and far between.

Your opportunities in the workforce today are the product of a series of slow, hotly contested political shifts that have occurred over the past 150 years. In my opinion, the most significant changes in labor force participation among American women—the dates and breakthroughs every American woman should know—are as follows:

- The signing of the Emancipation Proclamation in 1863, declaring that "all persons held as slaves . . . shall be free," which was made the law of the land by the ratification of the 13th Amendment to the U.S. Constitution in 1865

- The adoption of Married Women's Property Acts, in some but not all of the states, starting in 1839 and continuing into the late nineteenth century. In states that didn't pass it, the old English laws of coverture still applied, meaning that a married woman who was not a slave was nonetheless "covered" by her husband and had no legal status, including no right to own property. If she received a paycheck, those hard-earned dollars became her husband's property. The remnants of coverture were still in place in America as late as the 1960s, when many banks wouldn't loan money to unmarried women, and a wife's credit card was issued in her husband's name. The Equal Credit Opportunity Act, enacted in 1974, made that requirement illegal.

- The ratification of the 19th Amendment to the U.S. Constitution in 1920. Women had the right to vote in certain local elections before 1920, but the 19th Amendment expanded women's voting rights from sea to shining sea.

- The Supreme Court decision in Brown v. Board of Education in 1954, which began leveling the playing field in education

- The passage of the Civil Rights Act of 1964, which made it illegal to discriminate based on "race, color, religion, sex, or national origin" in schools, the workplace, and other public places, building on the Equal Pay Act of 1963. In 1972, Title VII was amended under the Equal Opportunity Act, ensuring that the EEOC watchdog could oversee enforcement.

- The enactment of Title IX of the Education Amendments Act of 1972, which outlawed the practice of excluding women from participating in educational programs on the basis of gender

- The adoption of the Lilly Ledbetter Fair Pay Act of 2009, which essentially eliminated the 180-day statute of limitations for pay-discrimination lawsuits

African American Women's Work: A Shared History

With the exception of the Emancipation Proclamation, which directly affected only women who were enslaved, the reforms I just described paint a picture in which all American women were vulnerable to injustice. Some historians note that in many tribes, Native American women enjoyed considerable equality to the men in their communities, only to see it taken away by European colonizers. Female Irish immigrants were often relegated to the lowliest of household jobs for no wages, working for many years to pay off the bonds incurred when they sought passage to America. Many of our Latina sisters, especially in the southwest, have experienced the double insult of being labeled "foreigners" on land that their ancestors settled long before the Mexican-American War. The few Asian women who came to America in the nineteenth century were sometimes brought against their will, smuggled in to serve Chinese miners during the California Gold Rush. At the same time, a White, well-educated upper-class wife had to contend with the fact that she had no separate legal existence from her husband, and if she inherited money from her family or had earnings through other means, every penny of it was technically her husband's property—and she had no voting power to enact change.

As grim as our shared history is, it is equally a history of triumph. Yet the history of Black women in America contains a distinctly harrowing element: centuries of slavery. No matter where your ancestors originated, it is important for all Corporate Sisters to understand the narratives of our shared histories. A global sisterhood is a force to be reckoned with, and a reckoning is due because the aftershocks of the slave trade, which stretched far beyond the Old South (including South America and my native Guyana), continue to reverberate; human bondage still thrives in the hidden form of human trafficking.

That is why I want to briefly describe the effects of the African slave trade. It's the story of my ancestors who arrived in Guyana two centuries ago, and there is much for all women in corporate America to glean from the special sisterhood of African American women. Until recently, most studies regarding slavery in the United States were about men. Few researchers have deeply examined the lives of female slaves, possibly because male slaves outnumbered them by a ratio of 60:40. We do know that many female slaves were traded to nontraditional plantation systems with such aspects as domestic concubines, slave preachers, slave overseers and many other societies within societies where toiling of the land was not the only form of slavery.

In terms of dollar value, the price of female slaves was on average much higher than for men because of a woman's ability to give birth to additional human commodities. This in turn led to horrific personal living circumstances for her; she lived in constant danger of being sexually assaulted and/or losing her family and her children. Her options were to revolt, submit, or run. Gwyn Campbell, a professor at McGill University in Montreal, has published eye-opening findings on this topic, and the scholarly journal Slavery and Abolition was part of my doctoral reading. As I accessed technology in my climate-controlled room, I always felt moved by the extraordinary difference between my life and the lives of the women described in my historical research.

The reality for slave women was to exist in two worlds: the master's household and the slave community. That sense of "dual membership" will resonate with many of you, I suspect. As a slave girl came of age, play transitioned into chores, and she might spend much of her time being trained by the mistress of the house, even sleeping on the bedroom floor of her mistress (who would expect her to take care of the early-morning chores before the family awoke), deprived of even the most precious mother-child rhythms of bedtime and waking together.

North of the Mason-Dixon line, White and Black women were joining to fight for abolition, which was interwoven with the fight for women's right to vote. Although they collaborated, there was still clear racism toward Black women. The most striking example of this (an example that illustrates the importance of a Corporate Sisterhood that transcends culture) was the rejection of Sojourner Truth at the National Women's Rights Convention of 1852, where she overcame resistance and was ultimately allowed to deliver what would become her renowned "Ain't I a Woman?" speech.

The conflict between White and Black female activists escalated in 1870 with the passage of the 15th Amendment, which granted Black men the right to vote (though violent acts of voter suppression made it largely a symbolic amendment, until the Voting Rights Act was passed in 1965). The 15th Amendment infuriated White women who did not expect Black men to receive the right to vote before they did. These first-wave feminists began aligning themselves with White men, rather than with Black women, in attempting to reach their political and social goals.

After the Civil War, multiple Civil Rights Acts were passed, but gender discrimination was not part of the language; instead, the acts focused on race, color, national, origin, and ethnicity, though enforcement (especially in the deep South) was scant. It took another a century (and the wrath of indignant Black GIs who had liberated Europe, only to return home and be treated as less than human) for a new Civil Rights movement to gain a true foothold. Most of the names you know from that movement are men's names; Rosa Parks is one of the few women who received notoriety, despite the fact that other Black women actively participated. A second wave of feminism was gaining momentum, but the needs of Black women were still not a top priority, and White feminists were more often the face of the movement. In response to this, a biracial political activist named Frances Beal helped to launch the Black Women's Liberation Committee (a caucus of the Student Nonviolent Coordinating Committee), which evolved into the Third World Women's Alliance to ensure the promotion of a political agenda for Black Women.

Are we reaping the rewards of those efforts in the twenty-first century? In many ways, Black women have made minimal progress into key positions of power and influence, struggling to move out of low-paying, low-status jobs. In 2008, the U.S. Census Bureau reported on pay variance between African Americans and their White counterparts.

Comparing those who shared the same level of higher education, Blacks earned approximately $9,000 less without an advanced degree and $21,000 less with an advanced degree. This disparity leads to exclusion and disengagement, but it has also given rise to a remarkable sisterhood of African American women in the corporate world. I'll share their stories later in this book.

Next Steps: Finding a Shero

Whether you turn to the pages of a history book or the stories of your own family, it's time to get personal and select your very own Shero. Regardless of which option you choose, it's important for you to know as much as you can about your personal women's history—

the legacies that are part of your own family lineage—even if you aren't able to trace that history very far back. When you look at those stories of sisterhood on the pages of history books (or history websites, or history shows on television), you need to know as much as you can about how your ancestors were affected by those events.

If you don't already know much about the women in your family history, it's time to start asking your relatives and digging to find old pictures and letters. If you were raised by someone other than your biological mother, you may not be able to gain access to the facts about your "genetic family," but you can try to get to know the history of those who raised you. If these personal histories turn out to be stories of brokenness or disappointment, there are nonetheless powerful lessons in those stories. You can make it your mission to heal your heritage, drawing on the strength of Corporate Sisterhood to move your family forward and become a source of inspiration for the next generation of daughters, nieces, and cousins.

It doesn't matter whether you choose to make your Shero your mother, your great- great-great aunt, your first boss, Cleopatra, Jennifer Lopez, Oprah Winfrey, Madam C. J. Walker (the first female self-made millionaire in America), Jackie Kennedy, or Dr. Mae Jemison (think NASA: she was the first Black female astronaut, born in the 1950s in Alabama, where Governor George Wallace delivered his "segregation forever" speech). You see my point: regardless of your ancestry, if you're a woman, you're surrounded by greatness! Welcome to the club.

Once you have selected your Shero—and you can certainly change Sheros throughout your lifetime, as you grow and evolve— you need to create an inventory of facts about her so that you can have her in the forefront of your mind, in detail. Find out the answers to these questions, comparing her life to yours every step of the way:

1. What was the world like when she was born? What were her greatest opportunities and her greatest adversities?

2. Who were her mentors and educators? Who were the members of her own sisterhood?

3. When she set about achieving her dreams, exactly how did she make it happen? If she seems to have just been "lucky," push yourself to understand what she did to appreciate and maximize that luck. How did she make the most of what she was given, no matter how meager it may seem by your standards?

4. What are the qualities you most admire about her?

5. What would she advise you to do about the current dilemmas you're facing?

If you like, you can keep her picture readily available on your desk or your phone or in your wallet. It's also OK to just picture her in your mind's eye; Corporate Sisters passed on their legacies to each other through storytelling and imagination long before the dawn of photography.

Portrait of Power: Dr. Maya Angelou

One of my Sheros is Dr. Maya Angelou. Her incredible life fills many books: she wrote multiple autobiographies, capturing various chapters in her life, and her labor spanned everything from being the first Black woman to work as a cable car conductor in San Francisco (she was not afraid of hard work and did whatever was required to support herself and her son) to serving as a professor at Wake Forest University for more than twenty-five years and immersing herself in acting, poetry, dance, and always the power of storytelling. I admire her because she debunked stereotypes and was a risk taker. I was once told, "history belongs to the risk takers." Dr. Angelou exemplified that of one who knew her power, but was keen on not allowing it to dull the light of others. She knew her strengths as well as her limitations, and equally important was the way in which she lifted as she climbed— extending herself to sisters of all races and religions around the world. When I first read her most famous book, *I Know Why the Cage Bird Sings*, dealing with strength, character, coming of age, and finally LOVE overcoming the challenges of racism and trauma, I was overwhelmed and inspired. Dr. Angelou didn't fold in the face of adversity even after becoming a teenage mother: she triumphed! That's why her words are the epigraph of this book.

Angelou was born in 1928 and spent her childhood in Stamps, Arkansas: a difficult time and place for a young African American girl, but she seemed to perceive no limitations. She cherished her grandmother, who was a force to be reckoned with, and eventually lived in Egypt and Ghana, mastering multiple languages (including Arabic and Fanti, a West African language). She gave voice to the voiceless, most powerfully in *I Know Why the Caged Bird Sings*, which revealed the sexual abuse that left her mute as a child. Her famous poem "Phenomenal Woman" is yet another distinct piece of work and anthem for many women wanting to derive strength, courage, and the spirit to walk tall as you enter any room as you please. At the time of her death in 2014, she had earned the Presidential Medal of Freedom and received more than 50 honorary doctorates. Whenever I have a day that feels like an uphill climb, I can find inspiration in her words and her journey. As she says in *A Song Flung Up to Heaven*, her memoir of the Civil Rights era, "We had come so far from where we started, and weren't nearly approaching where we had to be, but we were on the road to becoming better."

Dr. Jacque's Power Prescription #2

Choose an ancestor or historical figure who triumphed, and make her your personal role model. In essence, choose your Shero.

Personal Reflections

Choosing a Shero shouldn't be taken lightly. Think about Sheros you may have chosen in the past, or those who may be your Shero today. If your Shero is a source of strength for you, take time to thank her. If she's not meeting the true characteristics of a Shero, it may be time for a change. Whatever you do, choose wisely.

Three

What Dr. Jacque's Research Revealed

My Motives

The "D.M." after my name stands for Doctor of Management, in my case with a specialization in organizational leadership. As I mentioned previously, I was interested in learning more about the phenomenon of African American women who stick together on the job and use their networks effectively to advance up the ladder. I wanted to uncover the faces behind those statistics by conducting in-depth interviews. Along the way, I discovered many themes about the role sisterhood plays in overcoming challenges—themes that any woman in corporate America could apply to her own journey, regardless of her ancestry.

Even though the experience of women in corporate America can be viewed through a single lens, it's important to remember that workplace relationships between African American women are distinctly rooted in our ability to endure gender discrimination as well as racial oppression. Yale sociology professor Ron Eyerman (notably, a white male who earned his doctorate in Sweden) has studied this history extensively, and his book Cultural Trauma: Slavery and the Formation of African American Identity was one of the most harrowing and most interesting sources for my background research.

I could identify with his observation that Black women today often feel unsure of their worth, self-respect, and dignity as human beings.

This distinction in identity is significant because when we define ourselves and one another, race tends to take precedence over gender. That's why I set out to explore how the concept of sisterhood influences attitudes, shared culture, and experiences as perceived specifically by African American women leaders. I narrowed the scope even further by focusing on the Information Technology (IT) industry, in which I had been steeped for more than a decade. Another reason to focus on IT was the fact that women (of all races and ethnicities) are in the minority in the technology sector. "Women in Tech," an article published on CNet in May 2015, cited the findings of eleven of the world's largest tech companies, which calculated that women comprise only about 30 percent of the workforce in the tech industry, even though women make up 59 percent of the U.S. labor force. That has an impact on women's earning power, since technology jobs consistently rank among the highest-paying positions in America.

My Methods

After receiving approval from the institutional review board at my university, I used email to recruit sixteen African American women living in the Southeastern region of the United States (because that's where most of my contacts who held various corporate leadership roles lived) ranging from women who led others to program managers. I used my own professional network to find participants, and I selected them based on their positions within their organizations, as well as their active participation, experiences, and knowledge tied to sisterhood relationships. I also restricted the group to women who had ten or more years of corporate experience. They also needed to possess an enthusiasm for sharing their experiences. If you're wondering if this is like "stacking the deck," in fact my approach is widely accepted for this type of research question; it even has a name: purposive sampling, in which a researcher begins with a goal in mind and then selects the sample population that will best serve that purpose.

To create a common language in the study, I needed a consistent definition of leadership and sisterhood. I gleaned my definition of leadership from Wilfred Drath, director of the Center for Creative Leadership. He describes leadership as the nature of influencing others, as well as the process behind it and the outcomes that result from it. "Sisterhood" has many varied meanings in this book, but when I embarked on my study, I returned to the activist bell hooks (whose books are some of my most beloved); she has used the term "sisterhood" exclusively to refer to associations among African American women.

My next step was to pilot-test a questionnaire and then, after tweaking it for perfection, I used it to conduct digitally recorded telephone and face-to-face interviews, which I later transcribed. All of the participants signed a consent form, acknowledging that the findings might be published, and I promised to keep their identities anonymous. In the final tally, participants ranged in age from thirty-five to fifty-five and included a finance practitioner, an executive director, two executive assistants to vice presidents, four human resource practitioners, four program managers, one senior change practitioner, one senior customer service manager, one senior diversity consultant, and one marketing director. Nine of them held an M.B.A., and one had earned a Ph.D. All of them had completed a bachelor's degree.

You're probably eager to know what I asked these accomplished women. Here is the complete questionnaire. I encourage you to answer it yourself, writing down your responses so that you can compare yourself to other Corporate Sisters. You can adapt some of the questions, depending on how you define your Sisters.

1. In which age range do you fall?

   a. 35 to 44
   b. 45 to 54
   c. 55 to 64
   d. 65 and over
   e. Rather not say

2. What is your highest level of education?

   a. High School
   b. Some College
   c. Bachelor's Degree
   d. Master's Degree
   e. Doctorate

3. Have you experienced a sisterly relationship in your workplace or in your career?

4. What does sisterhood mean to you?

5. In your opinion, to what extent have these (sisterly) relationships aided your career advancement?

6. In your opinion, is it easier for you to form sisterly relationships with African American women than it is for you to form relationships with women of other races or ethnicities? What makes it easier or more difficult?

7. When you hear the phrase "shared culture," what comes to mind and what does it mean to you?

8. What customs, beliefs, values, or behaviors, if any, do you think African American women share?

9. What customs, beliefs, values, or behaviors affect the development of relationships between African American women?

10. What does spirituality mean to you? Does spirituality play a role in your relationships?

11. What bearing do you feel shared culture, history, and varying degrees of spirituality have on the bond of sisterhood?

12. Recognizing that women are unique in many ways, how are the relationships between African American women different from the relationships between African American women and other racial/ethnic groups?

13. Is it important to you that organizational leaders understand the relationship between African American women? If so, why?

14. Is your leadership style one of the following?
    a. Charismatic Leadership
    b. Servant Leadership
    c. Transactional Leadership
    d. Shared Leadership
    e. ransformational Leadership

15. What is the prevailing leadership style in your current organization's culture?
    a. Charismatic Leadership
    b. Servant Leadership
    c. Transactional Leadership
    d. Shared Leadership
    e. Transformational Leadership

16. What advice would you give to African American women aspiring to reach top leadership positions in Corporate America?

17. What advice, if any, would you give to organizational leaders regarding the relationships shared between African American women and the impact those relationships may have on organizational outcomes?

My Top Five Findings

As expected, my participants reinforced the findings of previous studies indicating that African American women who stick together, rise together in corporate America. What I did not expect was the degree to which common themes would emerge regarding how and why this sisterhood phenomenon occurred. And when I say "common themes," I mean that 100 percent of the respondents brought up the following themes. I excluded the themes that were mentioned less than 100 percent from this book so that we could focus on the true refrains. At the end of this chapter, you'll get to hear from some of these wise women themselves. Note: You might find question #15 about leadership styles helpful to you in discerning your own approach to leadership, but in my research study, respondents generally said that they operated with a mixture of styles, even if those styles didn't jibe with the corporate culture. There were no clear correlations between leadership styles, approaches to sisterhood, and organizational effectiveness.

For your next steps, think about what the following top five themes mean for you personally. How can they help you form, join, or enhance Corporate Sisterhood at your place of work?

1. *Unspoken Bond and Trust.*
Every participant expressed the belief that sisterhood is about a relationship based on deep trust, including open listening, having each other's back, and working with someone who cares. Every participant also underscored the fact that sticking together with other African American women helped raise the status of the group members because sisterly relationships were an essential pathway to support, endorsement, and upward mobility.

2. *Common Culture, Similar Upbringing, Cultural Norms and Experiences*
All of the Corporate Sisters I interviewed stressed the importance of having a shared history, culture, and spirituality if the bonds of sisterhood are to deepen. Participants eagerly shared that sisterly relationships, family, social connectedness, African American culture, and the community were all important factors to them. At the same time, the need to be authentic was a theme also emphasized by the participants. They indicated that regardless of their status, they needed the freedom to remain authentic and bring their "whole selves" to work each day.

3. *Spirituality as an Enhancement in Relationships*
Unless you work for a religious organization, you might be thinking that the "two kingdom" mentality is essential at work (separating your spiritual life from your worldly one). Yet my participants

all described spirituality as a key to sisterhood because it is an underpinning of a common upbringing. The Corporate Sisters spoke at length about the emphasis on spirituality in their upbringing, ranging from early school years into adulthood. Spirituality helped to shape their character and provided them with a specific set of shared customs. Each participant was careful to point out that spirituality is not the only factor in building relationships, but it resonated as a critical element.

4.   *Broader Network, Higher Net Worth*
The Corporate Sisters emphasized the fact that a broad network requires deliberate intention and action: you have to build it. But if you do, they all agreed, it positively impacts your net worth. They noted their ability to be included in key opportunities, projects, and nominations to enhance their skill sets and capabilities. They ardently stated they were able to form relationships with others who may not have a shared values or beliefs, but the communal beliefs shared by their Black colleagues proved to be a stronger catalyst for trust.

5.   *Good Sisterly Relationships: The Key to Corporate Retention*
The takeaway from this theme is that it's far more important for organizational leaders to understand the workforce relationships shared by all women—not just African American women—and they all believed that inclusivity is imperative. Participants agreed that organizational leaders should invest time in understanding relationships shared by African American women, but they said it's not enough to stop there. The participants described the benefits of understanding the needs of all women, irrespective of race or ethnicity. When a company is at risk for losing its best female employees, other female colleagues do the yeoman's job of talking

them off the ledge and giving them incentive to stay, in the form of kindred groups and a sense of belonging. Networks of close friends at work can have a positive effect on an organization's retention effort, so I've devoted the entire next chapter to this topic.

Portraits of Power

Each of the women who participated in my study is a powerful dynamo in her own right. Here are some of their most encouraging, insightful words to inspire you on your journey.

"I am my sister's keeper, and I have an obligation to cleave... When we stick together and help each other, we all win."—Leader #5

*

"My work sisters . . . are my truth tellers. They call it like they see it. They tell me when I'm messing up and when they're hearing good things about me. They give me an extra push, and because they support me, I don't want to let them down. In fact, I got my last role because a sista was looking out for me."—Leader #2

*

"A shared culture represents a common experience, such as the fact that so many of our mothers and grandmothers endured a struggle which we're still going through today as a people." —Leader #9

*

"Some of the things we share as African American women relates to the way we raise our families; our spirituality, going to church; and even some of the foods we eat. In addition, even our popular culture with traditional norms such as music and dancing shape our behaviors and values. The way we talk to each other is also unique. African American women are also very passionate... I think there is a perception of the 'angry black woman.' It's not that we're angry. We're just passionate. Passionate is who we are, and it drives us."—Leader #10

*

"We often work twice as hard as our counterparts, and most of us don't allow ourselves to fall behind. We focus on delivering our best every day."—Leader #7

*

"There are many days when I call upon my sisters to pray through an issue. Without a common spiritual foundation, that would not be possible. There is something special about having that kind of connection. It really helps on those tough days."—Leader #5

*

"I can think of someone I met years ago who shared the same beliefs and values as I do. She and I clicked, and the things we shared helped to develop our relationship. This is not to say that we don't ever encounter challenges in our relationship, but I think our history and experiences remind us of the unspoken bond and support that we should have for each other. . . . I can truly say that my broad network helps improve my net worth."—Leader#15

"I purposefully reach out to African American women who are new to my organization. Things that are unique to us help to further develop our bond because you feel that 'this is someone who knows what I'm up against on a daily basis, and she can relate to me and help me better myself.' When I reach out to up-and-coming African American women, the outcome is twofold: I help to improve my network, and they build theirs. The more people you know the greater possibility of expanding your net worth."—Leader #5

*

"God is at the center of my life. When I meet someone who shares my spiritual beliefs, it's a bonus to the relationship."—Leader #1

*

"Our history is our history. There is no denying it. It's like roots, and roots go deep. What was passed on to us and what we shared gives us a common understanding that helps to deepen the bonds."—Leader #10

*

"I know there is a God who is all powerful and knowing. It plays a role in my relationships, and it helps to shape my relationships by guiding it to a deeper place. With this common spiritual grounding, it's easier to hold people to their word as a result of our similar ethics and values."—Leader #3

*

"My sisters help to elevate me. We have a tendency to endure despite the odds because of our history, our culture, and our religious foundation. For most of us, giving up is just not an option."—Leader #11

*

"Speak up and ask for what you want. Plan or be planned for. This is so critical! The women who are successful in corporate America are religious about planning for the future. Sisters must find a way to take risks, be authentic, and still be able to fit in."

*

"What got you here, won't get you there. . . . Take some risks to improve and grow. African American women should also know their strengths and know when to toot their own horn, but when they toot, they must have supporters to back them up."—Leader #3

*

Dr. Jacque's Power Prescription #3

Each month, network with three individuals you don't know. Make sure your relationships are reciprocal. Always bring something to the table; don't just ask for help.

Personal Reflections

Network, Network, Network. Make your list and check it periodically to ensure you're connected with the right individuals.

-Four-

What the C-Suite Needs to Know

Why CEOs Should Care About Corporate Sisterhood

Anyone who's spent a long time in corporate America knows that "C" stands for chief: chief executive officer, chief financial officer, chief marketing officer, chief operations officer, chief communications officer. What would your work life look like if the "C" stood for compassionate? Caring? Competent? Coherent? How about champion—not only a champion in the sense of someone who is very successful, but champion as a verb: protecting and supporting the causes of others? The Corporate Sisterhood is poised to make that happen, infusing the chiefdom with holistic corporate health.

Since employee retention is critical to business success, the need to better understand the impact of sisterly workplace relationships is paramount. My research on African American female leaders underscores the positive effect on Black women who engage in these relationships, but the positive effect on the organization as a whole is equally significant. It is imperative that the C-Suite understand and encourage the Corporate Sisterhood. This "social capital" (described by Duke University sociology professor Nan Lin) provides the momentum for organizational growth. Lin's research has shown that the closer an employee is to a bridge within a network, the more success the relationship will bring forth. Access to social networks is vital for employees, and social relations and capital are critical elements in encouraging and maintaining a diverse, inclusive, and professional work culture.

If a woman attempts to break that glass ceiling by herself, she'll need a very tall ladder and a very big hammer—and she'll leave a pile of shattered pieces behind her. But if we work together, building bridges instead of ladders, we can remove that glass ceiling altogether, rolling it away instead of shattering it. The process should be like opening a window, bringing fresh air to the attic, without creating a single shard of broken glass.

In their book *Flex: The New Playbook for Managing Across Differences*, pioneering executive coaches Jane Hyun and Audrey Lee share the good news that the American workforce is "growing more multicultural, younger, and more female," along with the not- so-good news that "we are feeling the effects of the growing distance between frontline managers and workers from different backgrounds," which has an obvious impact on retention and productivity. Hyun and Lee put a price estimate on failing to retain employees, asking HR executives to calculate the costs of bringing employees onboard without providing meaningful development. The result? "Costs to replace an employee who has left to go elsewhere can range from 150 percent to more than double an employee's salary. That can amount to approximately $250,000 (including salary, recruiting, training, and onboarding) to replace a management consultant within the first year of hire after graduate school." In other words, the Corporate Sisterhood is worth its weight in gold!

Their research also indicates that a significant hurdle in retaining today's new hires is top-down culture where power is contained in the C-Suite instead of flowing freely, in both directions, through the "window." Despite its overlooked tangible value, Hyun and Lee also acknowledge the ways in which networking is sometimes misunderstood or discounted. They draw a comparison to China, where "you cannot do business unless you understand the importance of *guan xi* [relationship] and how to navigate the web of relationships." In contrast, corporate America is rife with bosses who see networking and relationship-building as a waste of time. "We see it play out with our gender differences as well," the authors write. "Men are often deemed as task-oriented and look for results in evaluating worth, while women place great importance on building trust first through establishing relationships—and often get good results by doing so."

One of my colleagues tells the story of a beloved female boss who survived a particularly difficult reorganization. She was asked by her new, male VP for spreadsheets showing how she analyzed the marketplace. She had plenty of data but told him that those spreadsheets were hardly her most valuable tool. "My secret weapon is lunch," she told him; the truly useful information (which had propelled her to the C-Suite) was gleaned from networking over lunch.

Far too often, the powers that be (C-Suite or not) will pass over an up-and-coming qualified woman, particularly a woman of color, because they haven't taken the time to invest in her, not only through training but by helping her to make the mental shift to a leadership identity. The next chapter of this book is devoted to promotions, but in this chapter I want to emphasize how managers factor into the equation. The women who are dependable, loyal, and smart, exceeding expectations on their metrics time and again, should be moving ahead. But they're often the ones who have their heads down, putting in the work and going above and beyond in every category except visibility. It's hard to see a single ant on the ground, but it's easy to spot a whole colony. That visibility is part of the power of networks, which are sometimes still seen as frivolous for women but a sign of influence in men.

Lastly, managers who realize how beneficial it is to increase gender diversity in upper management need to realize that creating a canned program or rote checklist will not solve the problem. A study titled "Women Rising: The Unseen Barriers" by Herminia Ibarra, Robin Ely, and Deborah Kolb, published in *Harvard Business Review* in September 2013, describes well-intentioned CEOzwho create goals for an increased proportion of female leadership and even develop training programs to achieve these goals, only to be frustrated to see that the pipeline of upwardly mobile women remains nearly empty. These researchers describe their key finding as follows:

> The problem with these leaders' approaches is that they don't address the often fragile process of coming to see oneself, and to be seen by others, as a leader. Becoming a leader involves much more than being put in a leadership role, acquiring new skills, and adapting one's style... It involves a fundamental identity shift... A significant body of research shows that for women, the subtle gender bias that persists in organizations and in society disrupts the learning cycle at the heart of becoming a leader. This research also points to some steps that companies can take in order to rectify the situation. It's not enough to identify and instill the "right" skills and competencies as if in a social vacuum. The context must support a woman's motivation to lead and also increase the likelihood that others will recognize and encourage her efforts—even when she doesn't look or behave like the current generation of senior executives.

The authors are describing a process of enhanced sponsorship, an important part of embracing the identity of leadership and being able to see ourselves in the role of chief. Remember that 100 percent of my respondents cited the correlation between having a network and being able to move around the organization to gain key experience. In addition, 100 percent of my participants emphasized the importance of sponsorship in ascending the corporate ladder. Sponsorship is very different from mentorship. As Leader #4 eloquently stated, "Building a solid network is important, but I will tell you that every new job or promotion that I received came because someone spoke up on my behalf. Throughout my career, I've had a few leaders who had my back and would always raise their hand to say, 'She should have that job.' A good network is helpful, but advocacy is critical."

An annual review of talent shouldn't stop with a score; a sponsor should be assigned to every high performer based upon her skillsets and capabilities. In the absence of formal sponsorship programs, you should actively seek out a sponsor who respects your authentic self, encourages you to take calculated risks, and will champion your cause. With that in mind, read on for my action plan.

Next Steps

We must change the narrative of how Corporate American is represented today. Here is a wish list, directed to our collective C-Suite.

1.   We need you to know that we're worth investing in. Put us in the succession planning pipeline. Give us the right mentors and sponsors, and we'll exceed your expectations.

2.   When we're given the opportunities, we do make things happen. Give us a platform, built on a level playing field, so that our achievements will be visible to upper management.

3.   Purge your mind of the ugly stereotypes regarding women, in particular women of color, and particularly African American women. Replace those falsehoods with our ability to scale and ultimately improve your bottom line.

4.   Appreciate our diversity and accept the benefits of inclusiveness, but bring us to the table in a meaningful way. Don't just make us visible; make us count! Bring us into the C-Suite with you so that we can in turn help you to create a truly diverse, talented pipeline of up- and-coming leaders.

5.   Create a culture that allows women to grow, thrive, and nurture their Corporate Sisterly relationships by building formal frameworks. These could include employee resource groups or advocacy groups geared specifically for key talent. And don't just build these groups—support them with your whole heart.

Portraits of Power

In the last chapter, I let you listen in on my conversations with leaders as they shared their observations about the power of the Corporate Sisterhood. Now I'll share their wisdom on the subject of what the C-Suite needs to know.

> "It's important for leaders to know we have a bond, but wondering why all the Black women are sitting on one side of the room should not be a focus. Honestly, we just like sitting together. Leaders should focus on the collective, not just on African American women. When I

connect with my sistas, it helps me deal with the corporate landmines a lot better. In a sense, corporate leaders need to know that my relationships at work keep me at work longer, and that helps the company with retention. In that sense, it's a bonus to understand us."—Leader #2

*

"As a businesswoman, I know the value of a good employee, and it wouldn't make sense to just focus on one group. If leaders do that, then we move a step backwards. So leaders should understand me, but at the same time, understand all women as well."—Leader #14

*

"Rethink grouping us as one. We do not all come in the same color or size. I truly believe that while we share many things in common, if they look at us individually, African American women can get a seat at the table. At the same time, I also want them to understand that the social aspect of sisterhood is important. Men don't call it a brotherhood, but there is a thing where men bond together. Social connectedness is very important in sisterhood, and learning how to do that well may benefit us individually and collectively."—Leader #6

*

"They have to understand the bond and the need to bring our entire selves to work: good, bad, or indifferent. . . . It's important for them to know that my family, the sisterly relationships I share, and the community are important factors in my life."—Leader #7

*

"With new organizational norms such as remote work and the like, organizations seem to care less about the ability to connect. Although I work remotely, I have an undeniable need to connect in person with my sisters. I make a point to do so at least once per month. When I see my sisters in person, given that we're often outnumbered in corporate America, it lifts my spirits. There is just something to the thought of that smile or nod of acknowledgement when I encounter a familiar face."—Leader #1

Dr. Jacque's Power Prescription #4

Don't lose your power, harness it. Identify the biases and misconceptions at your organization and make a game plan for becoming an agent for change. Find a sponsor, and be a sponsor.

Personal Reflections

Your purpose should drive your power! Take a few moments to reflect on the specific things that you will do, going forward, to fully harness your power.

-Five-

"Why Didn't I Get That Promotion?"

Now we get to the real reason you're reading this book. We're going to shift our focus from the big picture to a snapshot called YOU. If you've taken the initiative to read these chapters, that's already a sign that you're motivated to move up. But forming and joining a Corporate Sisterhood is no guarantee of success. You have to be willing to receive honest feedback from your sisters, and to be generous in helping them as well, if you're going to master the mentality of true leadership. Of course, if you have solid, copious evidence that the reason you weren't promoted is rooted in racism or sexism—or both—then you have three choices, and all three paths will require the support of your Corporate Sisters. You can turn your evidence over to the Human Resources department, or to the Equal Employment Opportunity Commission if HR is part of the problem, or to an attorney who specializes in employment law. Or you can turn your back on the organization and send out rescue signals to your network, striving to get hired by an ethical firm.

But if you're working for the good guys, and your career seems to have stalled, here are the top possible reasons why you're not moving ahead, along with the top ways in which your Corporate Sisters can help you overcome these obstacles:

1.   *You Don't Have Friends in High Places.* It's no secret that less qualified employees sometimes get the promotion simply because they have earned the trust of the hiring manager. Consider your Corporate Sisters to be like your very own board of directors. Recruit a combination of sisters who share your rank and those who are in higher-level positions with the power to promote you, because you're more likely to get promoted if your network includes decision makers and influencers. From within your network, seek out a sponsor. Remember that having a sponsor is even more important than having a mentor because a sponsor is someone with the power to grant your wish.

2.   *You're Not Honing Your Skills.* Note that I said "less qualified," not "unqualified" in tip #1. Even if you have friends in high places, that alone won't secure your future. Chapter seven of the gospel according to Matthew describes the difference between the wise man who built his house on the rock and the fool who built his on sand. The storyteller was referring to the dangers of false faith, but the metaphor applies to your livelihood as well. If you exploit your network to get a promotion for which you're unprepared and grossly underqualified, it will backfire, and you may have to wait a very, very long time before you'll be considered for a promotion again. Every promotion comes with a learning curve (and some learning curves are quite steep, with a steep salary to match) but every job requires fundamental skills that you need to master before applying for a promotion. Ask your Corporate Sisters to train you thoroughly and give you feedback about where you excel and where you're lacking. Never turn down opportunities for professional

development. Build your career on the rock of true proficiency, not the sand of mediocrity and illusion.

3. *You Haven't Developed a Cultural Compass.* If you have made friends with decision makers, and you've become so proficient that you're routinely rated as excellent on performance reviews, but you're still not getting promoted, it's time to consider the soft skills and unspoken factors that give some employees an advantage. This is where the true power of the Corporate Sisterhood kicks in, because you can glean facts that no careful supervisor would ever admit to your face if you asked why you were passed over for advancement. Your Corporate Sisters can tell you if your personality clashes with the culture of that particular team, or if your appearance is too conservative or too relaxed for that particular department of creative innovators, or if your impulsive, free spirit has led you to be perceived as unreliable. It's not about changing who you are in order to fit in with any given corporate culture. It's about getting real about who you are, and getting real about where the "real you" will excel.

4. *You're Invisible.* No matter how accomplished you are, power brokers won't know it if you continue to stand in the shadows, saying nothing in meetings, eating lunch at your desk, and keeping your ideas to yourself instead of sending that short, savvy email that showcases your genius thoughts. You may feel very uncomfortable receiving attention, and you may have been raised to believe that it's a sin to toot your own horn, but you'll never get ahead unless you stop being the invisible woman. Your Corporate Sisters can help you get comfortable with being seen and getting noticed. If you have to, take a class on how to toot but not brag. Find role models who can help you start basking in the limelight.

Next Steps

Building on the inventory you started in chapter one, start a lifelong Career Log. Use it to track your job titles and your compensation packages over the years. Update it every time you experience a change in either category. In the same booklet or e-document, keep track of your skills and other on-the-job assets, adding to the growing list each time you develop a new ability. Last but not least, keep track of your professional achievements, too, making note of how they added value to the company.

Use your Career Log to set specific goals for moving higher and higher, and make them SMART goals (specific, measurable, achievable, realistic, and time-bound). Don't accept offers of lateral moves without a specific strategy that leads to a more meaningful role.

Don't accept more work without more money and more status. Strive to land a promotion at least every two years. Here's some incentive, if you're worried that you might not be able to handle the responsibilities, risks, and workload associated with a promotion:

Waiting to move up can cost you hundreds of thousands of dollars in lost lifetime earnings.

Portraits of Power

The following portraits are drawn from my own Corporate Sisterhood. These are true stories, but I've changed the names to protect the privacy of my Sisters.

Shannon's Story

Shannon is an African American woman who graduated from the University of Florida with a Master's degree in Management. Prior to graduation, she spent two years interning at a Fortune 50 company and received glowing, positive feedback from her leaders during both years. Upon graduation, she was offered a full-time positon working for the very company where she interned. The challenge with her offer was that she was given a position three levels below what her skillsets and capabilities aligned to. In her case, advancement was going to be even more difficult because she was already behind on the starting line.

Telling herself that a low job was better than no job, Shannon accepted the position and thought she'd be able to propel herself out of that low-ranking zone through her sheer determination. Unfortunately, she ended up spending many years fighting to raise her valuation only to see newly minted college team members introduced to the organization and move into higher-level, higher-paying jobs. To make matters worse, she was consistently tasked with more complex work—even though she was passed over with promotions to match. This story has a happy ending, though. She remained loyal to the company and was eventually was promoted into a position closer to the one that she deserved, but it didn't come without "blood, sweat, and tears." She is currently one grade level off the appropriate mark where she should rightfully be.

How Did Shannon Finally Rise?

Shannon not only had to enlist the support of Human Resources, but she also needed to create her own "board of directors." She networked with anyone and everyone who would listen. When all seemed to be lost, she found a strong Corporate Sister who was promoted to executive director of HR. This person had been her long-time mentor and helped position Shannon appropriately in the eyes of decision makers. Today, Shannon understands the value of her network and the alignment to her *net worth*. Nonetheless, she is painfully aware that she must constantly stay in touch with her board of directors and keep her network of supporters engaged and informed.

The Lesson: Work with your Human Resources department, or make sure that someone on your personal board of directors can help you navigate HR.

Cathy's Story

Cathy is a hardworking, seasoned, African American professional in her fifties whose background is deeply rooted in the high-tech world. Cathy has been with her organization for close to two decades. Since joining her organization, she's only been promoted twice, while her male counterparts have been promoted to the executive ranks at a much faster pace. Cathy has a dual undergrad degree and an M.B.A. from a notable university in Texas.

During her annual reviews, she consistently receives positive feedback. Cathy also receives additional financial compensation in the form of long-term incentives—something only a small percent (usually 10 to 20 percent) of the organization's workforce receives. Shouldn't she just learn to be content with such a comfortable compensation package? Of course not! Yet Cathy is definitely stuck in what I call the "frozen middle." At the beginning of the book, I described the sizeable percentage of women who are in middle management. Cathy is one of those women. Given the backdrop of her reviews and financial incentives, one would ask, "Why hasn't Cathy been promoted to the *very* top?"

The responses she has received over the years have been devoid of anything substantive, which in turn has eroded her confidence. The cumulative effective of the micro-inequities that Cathy has endured have desensitized her to the point where she is having a hard time leaving her company. On one hand, she is handcuffed by the long-term incentives (which can be lucrative, given the three-year payout) that make it hard for her to consider working for other companies, but on the other hand, she is disenfranchised each time someone else gets promoted while she remains stagnant.

Today, Cathy continues to work hard and seem to have the ears of many senior leaders; however, I believe that years of hearing those old tapes in her head has put her in a position where she believes she is less than. Despite her M.B.A., she defers to those who have additional degrees or certifications. She finds ways to devalue herself in her own mind. Thus, she keeps her head down and continues to focus in the areas where she can add value without visibility or risk.

How Will Cathy Rise?

The good news is that Cathy finally took a small, proactive step in landing the leadership roles for which she is so clearly qualified. That step was to reach out to DR. JACQUE. I am helping her understand her position in the marketplace while culling hard-coded data regarding salaries, qualifications, and opportunities. Like most women in her position, Cathy is skeptical and worried that we're aiming too high. With determination, I know that I can shift her mindset. It's not enough to be grateful that you even have a seat at the table. Strive to sit at the head of the table.

The Lesson: Don't let the rewards of middle management make you so comfortable that you stop striving to reach the mountaintop. Watching others climb higher than you, even when you're working harder than they are, will erode your self-esteem, and your perquisites and benefits will not make up for the emotional damage. Reach out to a mentor or a sponsor who can look at your situation objectively and help you strategize to win First Prize.

Maria's Story

Maria is a brilliant Latina woman with more than ten years of experience in IT. She is a results-oriented and collaborative leader with influence across multiple geographies and cross-functional organizations. Maria had worked her way up the ranks doing everything she was asked to do, making a check mark for each task and role she was given. She pursued that dangling carrot of "soon and very soon," and she managed to escalate to the executive ranks. Maria even became the chief of staff for one of the top executives in her company. In fact, Maria's LinkedIn profile would make anyone become a bit green with envy. Yet, like most of the other women in her position, Maria was not able to scale the path all the way to the top within the company where she had spent more than a decade.

How Did Maria Rise?

This one was simple: Through the use of effective networking, leveraging male and female leaders, Maria was able to leave the organization and land a much higher-ranking position at a competing firm—a significant loss to her foolish former employer.

The Lesson: You may have to switch employers in order to make it all the way to the C-Suite. Many corporations fail to capitalize on the assets of their own in-house talent and insist on recruiting from outside the organization when they're looking to fill the top slots. Receiving promotions and raises doesn't obligate you to stay with a firm. If they're only rewarding you with a fraction of your true value, you only owe them a fraction of your loyalty.

Dr. Jacque's Power Prescription #5

Each month, review your personal and professional goals, and give yourself a reality check about what it will take to achieve them.

Personal Reflections

Your purpose should drive your power! Take a few moments to reflect on the specific things that you will do, going forward, to fully harness your power.

-Six-

What Men Can Do to Advance Our Cause

You're probably thinking, "I know what men can do to advance our cause: give us the promotions and raises we have earned!" They certainly have the power to do so: according to Catalyst, as of July 26, 2016, men hold 95.6 percent of the top positions at S&P 500 companies. But the challenges are daunting, especially in the lucrative tech sector. Software developer Rachel Thomas summarized a slew of these challenges in her widely circulated article, "If You Think Women in Tech Is Just a Pipeline Problem, You Haven't Been Paying Attention," published on medium.com in 2015. Thomas cites a randomized, double-blind 2012 study conducted at Yale by researchers in biology, psychology, psychiatry, and management (it's rare to see such an interdisciplinary team). They asked science faculty at six institutions to assess applications for a lab manager position. Female applicants were rated as being significantly less competent and hirable. Identical applications with male names were also deemed to deserve a higher starting salary and more career mentoring.

We're confronted by statistics—or experiences—of male bias all the time. But a book about Corporate Sisterhood won't be effective if we try to turn the tide of inequality all by ourselves. In fact, I don't think a book about advancement for women in corporate America is complete without an entire chapter dedicated to men. In the paragraphs that follow, I will share some of the ways men and women can begin to work together to ensure that all employees can thrive, achieving their true potential while helping the company achieve its true potential in a competitive global marketplace. Corporate Sisters, if you are fortunate enough to work for people like the ones I am about to describe, thank them, take note of all the things they're doing right, and strive to pass it on.

In case you hadn't noticed, my starting point is always gratitude, not attitude. I want you to meet three extraordinary men who exemplify the spirit of bridge-building. They understood that our differences and our common understandings worked together to create strong teams. I am grateful to them for not only coaching me and promoting me, but for serving as my role models. Here are a few leadership lessons from some of my male superheroes.

Jerry

One of the earliest mentors and leaders who inspired me in meaningful way was Jerry Maloney. Jerry was the Site Director at Aerial Communications (now a merged entity of T- Mobile USA). From the moment I met Jerry in my interview for a supervisory position, he told me he wanted me on his team, and he also told me that he saw exponential leadership capabilities within me. He invited me to join his team within a week of that meeting.

Jerry was keen on providing weekly feedback to me on the things I needed to do to enhance my effectiveness. He took the time to help me excel far above the average. Yet he also said he believed in me, and he trusted my abilities to do the job. He didn't micromanage; he empowered me to lead my team. Within ninety days, Jerry promoted me to Operations Manager. It's interesting to observe the dynamics of being a peer one day and then becoming the leader of your peers the next day. While this is tough transition for many who find themselves in this situation, Jerry made sure that I was fully supported when this became my reality. As I moved to my new role, Jerry continued to mold and inspire me like a peer, even though he was my boss. In fact, from my perspective, we developed a reciprocal relationship where we both coached each other. Jerry is now managing his own consulting firm in Missouri. I can still see his genuine smile, feel the warmth of his sincere kindness, and hear some of his inspiring and quirky "isms."

Once Jerry and I were conducting an interview and he became so tongue tied with his line of questioning that the candidate became so speechless due to lack of understanding and began laughing. The laughter didn't bother Jerry. Instead, he laughed and we all continued laughing. While this may seem silly, it's another illustration of a leader who could simply be human. We shared several experiences like the ones I just mentioned in the interview with Jerry. As time moved on, "Jerry Speak" became our fun little inside joke.

Rob

When I was ready for my next challenge (always strive to rise, Sisters!), I was fortunate enough to interview with Robert McIntosh at Dell, Inc. In contrast to Jerry, Rob has mastered the quintessential poker face, but even so, I felt his genuine spirit to serve when he interviewed me. More than willing to open that glass window a few inches, he hired me to be one of the first female call center managers for the Consumer Technical Support organization that existed in Austin, Texas, at the time. Like Jerry, Rob practiced what he preached. He gave me a job to do, and he gave me the freedom to do it well. He was an action-oriented guy who focused on results (he's now an executive director at Dell: see what I mean about results?).

It was good for me to see a leader exhibiting a different but highly effective communication style. He used about seventy-five percent fewer words than Jerry did, but our one-on-ones were purposeful and intentional. We focused on what key actions were being taken to drive results, what I was doing to make a difference in the call center, and what specific things would come next. He really helped me understand the power of SMART goals (specific, measurable, achievable, realistic, and time-bound). His quiet persistence was inspirational. He pushed me to excellence—which is very different from pushing an employee just to flaunt your power.

When I look back, he is clearly one of those people who "put their money where they see a sure win." But he was the kind of leader who was willing to share the dividends of that "investment." Under Rob's guidance, I was also promoted within four months from my start date at Dell. Yes, he believed in me that much. The promotion also illustrates that my capabilities were beyond the level of the job for which I was initially hired.

Unwittingly, he became partially responsible for my attaining my coaching certification in 2005. My interest in coaching was sparked because of a few words he uttered to me the year before: "You're a GREAT coach, Jacque." Later, Rob nominated and enlisted me into Dell's Key Talent program. In this program, a coach was assigned to me, providing me with all-important visibility to senior leaders, and providing me with sponsorship as well. It was that sponsorship which led me to transition from call center leadership. I moved into a new lane as a human resources practitioner, beginning with a niche in Diversity and Inclusion, and then later becoming an HR Business Partner.

What is also important to note about Rob is that even after I moved on from his organization, he continued to support and follow me. When I became the HR Director/Business Partner supporting the Chief Procurement Officer at Dell, I was glad to extend my body of knowledge in HR to benefit Rob, who also reported to the CPO.

Oprah Winfrey has a question that she often asks various leaders and personalities at the end of her interviews. The question is, "What do you know for sure?" (and she wrote a bestselling book called *What I Know for Sure*). What I know for sure is that Rob McIntosh is one of the people I can still count on today. I could pick up the phone and give him a call if there were a need, and he would have my back. He's just that kind of a leader. He's all about results, but he's fiercely loyal and has an equally big heart that inspires you to action!

Mark

The third executive who led me even higher on the ladder during those formative years is Mark Harris, also at Dell. (Mark has since transitioned from Dell to Amazon.) Like Jerry and Rob, he didn't withhold praise, and he celebrated excellence. Also like Jerry and Rob, Mark didn't really know me when he first interviewed me, but I can so clearly remember that after I spoke with him for thirty minutes, he leaned back in his chair with a level of confidence only Mark could project, smiling and saying, "Jacque, what you have and bring to the table is unlike what most of the HR Business Partners have, and that is breadth of experience." He spoke greatness into me with those words.

Mark went on to summarize my resume, saying something like, "I'm not sure if I can point to anyone else who has worked on Wall Street, served their country, worked the business [Dell's call centers], with Diversity and Inclusion knowledge, academic knowledge, and a sound understanding of people." Just the fact that he had taken the time to notice the details of my journey made me feel elated and made me want to give my best to the company. He went on to say, "It's also a big plus that you're passionate about people." He knew what mattered. Mark was also a great coach. Like the others, he didn't micromanage; he just had an expectation. Harvard Business School Professor Rosabeth Moss-Kanter has written extensively about the fact that empowerment is critical to employee satisfaction. Mark simply empowered me to do great work. Under Mark's leadership, I was once again promoted.

When I left Dell in 2013 to rise even higher in a different industry, the hardest thing for me to do was to tell Mark that I was moving on. He was not only an exemplary leader whom I trusted, but he also managed to remain a "salt of the earth" person: a good guy who cares about humanity. It is not by chance that everyone who worked for him felt the same way I did.

Next Steps

Consider the wisdom of the three leaders I have described in this chapter. Apply their techniques to foster confidence and excellence across gender lines throughout your organization:

1. When you've hired someone to do a job, you must allow them the space to ramp up appropriately, make mistakes, grow and thrive. In each of my roles, I wasn't perfect, but I was allowed the space needed to get into my zone.

2.   Give colleagues the freedom to bring their whole selves to work each day. These leaders understood that we all rise when we can be our authentic selves. I never had to quash my passion, my quirkiness, my drive, or my own colloquialisms. They accepted and celebrated my everything without judgement.

3.   Generously share your best practices while allowing others to inject their own. True leaders don't feel threatened when other people offer good ideas. In each of those three positions, I never doubted that I had been hired because my opinions and expertise were valued. This doesn't mean we always did everything my way. It means that my leaders were always on the lookout for that perfect combination of innovative solutions.

4.   Know the difference between coaching and counseling. The stereotype is that men make better coaches and women make better counselors. The reality is that all team members need some of each, and they're all capable of delivering both. That said, coaching is more challenging (and to some degree, more important to the corporate world) because it requires identifying and overcoming hurdles. I'm living proof that women can be strong coaches, and that good achievers can become great achievers if they receive first-rate coaching.

5.   This tip is for male leaders who, deep down, are silently skeptical that women can deliver the best results: Give yourself a reality check. Look at the statistics on profitability at companies that have diverse leadership. Give a qualified, motivated woman the chance, and empower her to do her job. You'll eventually see big dividends, which can create a ripple effect. Share the abundance.

6.   If you are a woman and feel daunted because all the VPs and C-Suite executives in your company are men, this last tip is just for you: Seek out leaders who are like Jerry, Rob, and Mark. Apply for positions on their team. Gravitate to true leadership, and show gratitude when they are willing to coach you.

Portrait of Power

For this chapter's portrait of power, I want to focus on my father, Roy Walters. When I was a young child, my grandfather told me that I was created with greatness, and greatness is what both my grandfather and father expected from me. My dad was short in stature but tall in wisdom. For years, I held on to some emotional baggage from the fact that he said he wouldn't attend any of my graduation ceremonies until I had earned my doctoral degree, but he sadly didn't live to see that day. Today, I realize he made statements like that in order to push me harder so that I could soar even higher than he had.

Although Dad did not have formal institutionalized education in the United States, he was one of the smartest men I knew. In fact, the entire Walters family is known for their strong academic knowledge. My father had an exemplary knack for numbers, literature, and architecture which, elevated him to high ranks as he oversaw several key projects as a foreman in our native Guyana. Later he worked at and retired from Downstate Medical Center (State University of New York) doing carpentry, construction, and facilitates engineering work. Without a doubt, my father garnered his pursuit of excellence from both his mother and father as he later attempted to go back to college while working full time. Unfortunately, Dad did not complete his college pursuits.

Despite those aspirations, I now understand that my dad was trying to raise a family in poverty. At the time, I didn't know how poor we were, but my biological sister was sent off to live with my grandmother; that was just one indication of not having enough income to feed all the mouths in our household. (Nonetheless, the bonds of sisterhood between my sister Sharon and me were finally shaped when we were in our teens and has grown stronger as we've matured.) Dad was strong as an ox and did what he could to support us, working dangerous construction jobs in Guyana and eventually moving all of us to Brooklyn, where he continued to work for Downstate Medical until his retirement.

One of the many things he taught me was that a strong man can have a happy marriage with an equally strong woman. He and Mom were true partners. I watched her make a dollar out of fifteen cents, working hard each day as a nursing assistant and keeping a clean house while making small meals stretch to feed a family of ten. Yet my parents never said anything that made us feel "less than." It never occurred to me to think about what I didn't have.

Best of all, Dad didn't discriminate against girls. As I mentioned earlier, I was the eldest daughter (third child in the ranks), which made no difference to him. There were five siblings behind me, and there was always much work to be done; somehow, I acted like the oldest of them all, not just the eldest daughter. My dad wanted all of his children to recognize their God-given, abundant resources— intellect and courage were at the top of the list—and I'm convinced that the blessing of having a strong, loving father paved the way for my success.

There are three lessons Dad imparted that I have returned to again and again. First, he would say things were anchored in a duality of life. On one hand, he wanted to give me incentive to excel, but he would also share the Guyanese saying, "Take your time and peel your pine," meaning, don't rush to get everything done (quality over quantity). Secondly, he was so dogmatic about reading that if he caught me just lounging around, he'd tell me to go read a book. Every time I opened a book, I was opening a door to a new world, and I thank him for giving me the gift of the printed word. Lastly, I'll forever remember his sage advice to "keep living." Those are very simple words, but at the core, they remind me that the more you live, the more you'll learn. When I earned my bachelor's degree, the keynote speaker said that when you become a learned person, you never see the world the same way again. As I think of those words, I think of my dad. Whether you're learning academically or otherwise, to live is to learn, and to learn is to rise.

Considering that men currently dominate the top jobs in corporate America, Corporate Sisters who have daughters would be wise to encourage connections with Dad or Grandad, if those men have a loving temperament. Based on my experience in the shadow of both a wonderful dad and grandad, I offer the following advice for today's father figures (I call it the ICONS approach):

1. INFORM your daughter about the harsh realities of the world, but let her know that you fully support her and will help her break down the walls that were once built to hold women back.

2. COACH your daughter to be more than she may believe she can be, and push her to find "mind over matter solutions" when she stumbles. Instill in her the belief that she can do anything she puts her minds to with the right level of effort and passion.

3.   OBSERVE your daughter's triumphs. Praise will not make her weak (quite the opposite is true, if she's truly triumphed). Don't be such a workaholic, or such a taskmaster, that you overlook her achievements. Be present for the ceremonies. Do the world's most audacious victory dance. Added bonus: Celebrating her victories will enhance *your* confidence—not just hers.

4.   NURTURE your daughters, speaking greatness into them just as you'd supply a seedling with water and sunlight.

5.   SHOW your daughters, not just through your words but by your actions, the things that you are personally doing to ensure that every little girl and every woman in the world has the freedom to reach her God-given potential.

Dr. Jacque's Power Prescription #6

Each month, network with three individuals you don't know. Make sure your relationships are reciprocal. Always bring something to the table; don't just ask for help.

Personal Reflections

Most of us have varying ways to share and show gratitude but far too often, we become caught up in the day-to-day grind and simply lose track of the importance of sharing and giving thanks. Reflect on how you've done in this area, and begin creating a new normal of personal sharing and gratitude. Go ahead, start your own gratitude phenomenon! Be sure to make notes and review this page as you see fit.

Seven

How Corporate Sisterhood Is Changing the Narrative

This book brings to light the benefits of Corporate Sisterhood on net worth, self-fulfillment, and a corporation's bottom line. But on May 22, 2008, I discovered that Corporate Sisterhood has an even more important benefit. That's the date of my breast cancer diagnosis. It's still difficult for me to think about that day, and the rough months that followed. During the previous month, I completed my well woman exam with an A+ passing grade—meaning all organs, blood work, and associated systems were working extremely well. Two weeks after my annual exam, I felt a lump in my left breast that seemed abnormal because it wasn't there in the months prior. My lump seemed so out of place that I felt compelled to call my doctor. My frantic call was met with the tone that I was overanalyzing; something couldn't possibly be there given the fact that my annual breast exam showed no signs of abnormal tissue. Thanks to my sharp instincts, I refused to go away quietly and forced my doctor's hand in ordering a mammogram. I was scheduled for a routine screening weeks later.

Subsequently, after waiting for like what seemed an eternity, my mammogram exam was scheduled for May 19, 2008. The routine mammogram, which would normally take an estimated thirty minutes, took about two hours. All I can remember is the radiologist coming into the dressing room and sharing with me that he was sorry for the wait—he had already placed a call to my doctor because the tissue he saw looked abnormal, and my films were being couriered over to my doctor and a surgeon concurrently. The scene was very dramatic. Before the day was over, I was talking to my primary care physician and seeing a surgeon within a four-hour time frame.

What I know for sure is that in order to thrive, Corporate Sisters need to stay alive! That means getting mammograms every year and staying current with your other health screenings too. Make your health a priority. If you're someone who takes better care of her car than her body, you should explore the reasons behind this and start putting your health first.

I was one of the "lucky" ones, thanks to early detection and my instincts: stage 1A (the breast tumor was no more than two centimeters, or no more than three-quarters of an inch across, and the cancer had not spread to the lymph nodes). I was determined not to experience fear; I placed my trust in God and was certain I could send that tumor straight to hell. But there was no denying that I was facing a grueling journey of surgery, chemotherapy and radiation. Part of me wanted to quit my job, buy a plane ticket back to the Caribbean, and turn my treatment into a holiday. I had no idea how I would fare, but I did know that my body was otherwise extremely fit and ready to take what was about to come. The other part of me did not want cancer to jeopardize my livelihood and disrupt all I was achieving at work. This experience taught me the most meaningful benefit of Corporate Sisterhood: We're not robots. In order for us to keep going, maintenance of body, mind, and spirit—on the job and when we're off-duty—takes teamwork.

My personal Corporate Sisterhood really began when I enlisted in the Unites States Army and later extended to a broader-based sisterhood when I joined the illustrious membership of Delta Sigma Theta Sorority, Inc., a public-service sorority that traces its roots back to Howard University. My thirty sisters who were initiated into Delta with me will forever share a bond unlike any other, and I will forever be grateful for the bonds of our sisterhood. You may recall my Army memories of being in Korea with Terri, Desiree, and Shawn. After my cancer diagnosis, the bonds of sisterhood extended for me with three additional soul sisters; Dawnita, Angela, and Darlene. These were my Dell sisters who stepped in and said, "Whatever you need, we're here for you." While I was strong in my convictions, I could not have made it without of support of these three amazing women.

When I was fighting cancer, I formed a "war room" in my head (and on the phone), enlisting a small group of sisters from all aspects of my life, which included my Dell Sisters, even though I was torn between letting people know what I was going through and wanting to hide this deeply personal challenge. It required a very special team. Here are a few of the ways in which that particular Sisterhood carried me to the finish line of healing and total wellness:

1.   They prayed for me each day. Not one day went by without someone calling to pray or check in.

2.   They showed up, physically and spiritually, extending their time and resources to support my needs. Through my network of sisters, I was blessed with a housecleaning service for 6 months—a much-needed resource when faced with neuropathy in my fingers.

3. My sisters cheered me up when I was down and also made sure that if I needed help with my work, I had their support. In essence, they had my back.

Again, belonging to the Corporate Sisterhood does not mean that we fail to honor the men who have honored us. Words cannot express how much of a support and cheerleader my husband, Patrick Colbert, is to me. Although I met my husband after my battle with cancer, finding a man like Patrick felt like a sweet reward, and my illness gave me a deeper appreciation for love. Some men (and women) have trouble expressing love. Not Patrick. He said, "I love you" on the day we met! But Patrick is not one to just talk (and trust me, he likes to talk). He's also a man of action. If he says it, he can back up his words. Neither of us is perfect, but he understands the plight of women across the world, and he understands some of the things we often face in the workplace. It is not by chance that he works in an environment where ninety-five percent of the organization is female. He also has a unique insight as the oldest child, with four younger sisters.

I love him for many reasons, but perhaps the most refreshing thing about him is that he is not threatened by my drive to do the work that I desire to do, and that I was meant to do. When God sent Patrick to me, He sent someone who empowers me by making me smile brighter and stand up taller, and he gave my heartsong a new tune. I wish every Corporate Sister had a Patrick by her side, but I know too well that he is a rare gem.

I am better today because of the love, support and empowerment I receive consistently from my favorite guy, but many of you may be in relationships that have the opposite effect, draining you of your confidence and your sense of self-worth. If that's the case, having a Corporate Sisterhood will make it easier to face the reality and let go of a situation that is impeding your ability to thrive. Don't settle for a relationship with someone who doesn't treat you with love and respect. You will stand stronger alone than with a person who tries to undermine your happiness. But Patrick is proof that there are wonderful guys out there, and I believe that well-adjusted people attract each other. Your Corporate Sisterhood can help you build your confidence and also introduce you to great catches. If you are as fortunate as I was, you know it's worth the wait.

Looking to the Future

Being a survivor has transformed the way I view the world. It has put me on a mission and given me a new vision for improving the working lives of all women, including my precious daughter's generation. I celebrate each day not just as a survivor but as a "Thriver." It's not enough to just survive; I want to flourish and grow, and I want my Sisters to do the same. I believe that history belongs to the risk takers, and for me that means I must wake up every day full of cheer as my dear husband would say; ready to face the world, giving of myself to make a difference. The truth is, I've always been an easy-going full of life person, but having lived through and conquering cancer while honoring the memories of those who didn't make it—I've got a job to do!

I am confident that our Sisterhood is changing the narrative of corporate America because of all that I have seen since I took that subway train to Wall Street when I was just a teenager. Yes, the shift is slow, but I've seen some movement for women in corporate America. For the first time in our history, we have a female nominee for President of the United States of America, *and* whether you like her or not, she is the first. I'm also encouraged by the likes of Ursula Burns, who has been at the helm of Xerox since 2009 and has risen through the leadership ranks from the level of intern in 1980, transforming Xerox from a global leader in documents to the world's most diversified business service company.

In addition to Burns, I'm also encouraged by the brilliance of Indra Nooyi, who remains a strategic force for PepsiCo. Why do I say I'm encouraged? I'm encouraged because women CEOs are proving that they have as much staying power as their male counterparts. As a naturalized U.S. citizen, Nooyi has shown that irrespective of your background, a woman with the same credentials as a man can make a difference if given the chance.

Along those same lines, I'm equally encouraged by the likes of Carly Fiorina, the first woman to lead a top 20 company—a high-tech company at that. If I were to guess, I'd say she's not quite done making waves. While we're at it, let's not forget the force that is the honorable Sonya Sotomayor, the first Latina woman to ascend to the level of U.S. Supreme Court justice! From a not-so-traditional perspective, I'm also encouraged to see African American women such as Shonda Rhimes, the writer, television producer, and screen writer who rules ABC television on Thursday nights with a jammed packed line-up of *three* successful shows, in an industry often "owned" by men.

I AM encouraged! Each of these women has been named on lists of the world's most influential women. Finally, I am also encouraged by the immutable surge in the number of female entrepreneurs who are re-defining what success looks like: the bloggers, Corporate Fashionistas, mompreneurs and the like. I am encouraged by their passion and their work. So while there is still much work to be done, I am encouraged that even a woman like me, born in a country most people may not have even heard of, has the opportunity to use my voice to make a difference in the lives of others. I AM ENCOURAGED!

Next Steps

Why have things improved? Progress always starts with a vision of the future, followed by a single action that helps build traction. I have never achieved something that I did not first envision, asking God to inspire me every step of the way. For your final assignment, answer the following two questions:

1.   What is your personal vision for the future of your Corporate Sisters? Be detailed, describing the changes you would like to see, depending on your industry.

2.   What actions can you take this week, this month, and this year to turn that dream into reality?

Portrait of Power

The final spotlight goes to Jane Cooke Wright, M.D. Never heard of her? She would probably want it that way. Her humility kept her from being a household name, but she received significant recognition during her lifetime for being a pioneer physician and cancer researcher who helped launch the field of oncology. In fact, she was a founding member of the American Society of Clinical Oncologists (ASCO) in 1964. What's more, she was the only woman among the charter members of ASCO, and she was one of the few African American physicians conducting clinical cancer research at the time. According to the Kaiser Family Foundation, in 2015 the number of women versus men graduating from American medical schools was almost equal (8,907 women compared to 9,798 men) but that was hardly the case seventy years ago, when Jane graduated with honors from New York Medical College. Today, a female med student like Jane would enjoy a much more visible Sisterhood.

What did it take for a Black woman born in 1919 to become a world-renowned oncologist, leading delegations to Africa, China, and the Soviet Union, seemingly isolated in a field dominated by men? Intelligence, courage, passion, and drive, of course. But it won't surprise you to know that she had the lifelong encouragement of her high-achieving father, Louis Tompkins Wright, one of the first African American graduates of Harvard Medical School. In 1949, long before the Civil Rights Act was passed, she joined her father at Harlem Hospital, where he was director of the Cancer Research Foundation. Teaming up with her dad, she performed patient trials using an experimental treatment— chemotherapy—for leukemia and cancers of the lymphatic system. After her father died three years later, she was appointed head of the foundation at the young age of thirty-three. Three years after that, ever rising, she became director of cancer chemotherapy research at New York University Medical Center.

Nine years later, Lyndon Baines Johnson tapped her to serve on his Commission on Heart Disease, Cancer, and Stroke. By 1967, she was a professor of surgery and head of the Cancer Chemotherapy Department at her alma mater, New York Medical College, at a time when there were only a few hundred African American women physicians in the country. She didn't let the demands of her career keep her from raising two daughters with her husband, an attorney. She lived to be ninety-three years old.

Jane's *New York Times* obituary included a quote from an interview that she gave to the *New York Post* in 1967. She told the reporter, "I know I'm a member of two minority groups, but I don't think of myself that way. Sure, a woman has to try twice as hard. But— racial prejudice? I've met very little of it. It could be I met it—and wasn't intelligent enough to recognize it." Buried in that self-deprecating comment is a brilliant statement of wisdom. We all know the reality of the world she inhabited, and we all know the horrific headlines and television news images she couldn't have avoided, reminding her of the risks she faced. She could never have imagined that 8,907 women would follow in her footsteps and graduate from fully integrated American medical schools in 2015. But she was intelligent enough to recognize that no matter how daunting the cast of characters in her profession might have looked, just like Maya Angelou's moons and suns she could choose to focus on rising, higher and higher, performing extraordinary work that would save the lives of her fellow human beings, even into the twenty-first century.

Dr. Jacque's Power Prescription #7

Take time to mentor, even if you're in an entry-level job; sisterhood thrives on giving as much as you receive. Let's lift as we climb. As you grow and thrive, reach back to enrich the lives of others.

Dr. Jacque's Power Prescriptions for Every Working Woman

As you continue to rise, be encouraged and keep the seven power prescriptions in mind. Whenever you need a refill, just refer to this page:

#1: Become your own Human Resources Director, continually researching the facts about your individual job market, your marketability, and broader shifts that affect your livelihood.

#2: Choose an ancestor or historical figure who triumphed, and make her your personal role model. In essence, choose your *Shero*.

#3: Each month, network with three individuals you don't know. Make sure your relationships are reciprocal. Always bring something to the table; don't just ask for help.

#4: Don't lose your power, harness it. Identify the biases and misconceptions at your organization and make a game plan for becoming an agent for change. Find a sponsor, and be a sponsor.

#5: Each month, review your personal and professional goals, and give yourself a reality check about what it will take to achieve them.

#6: Ladies, share this chapter with the great men in your life, and thank them for being part of the solution. Gratitude goes a long way.

#7: Take time to mentor, even if you're in an entry-level job; sisterhood thrives on giving as much as you receive. Let's lift as we climb. As you grow and thrive, reach back to enrich the lives of others.

See you at the TOP! Your Corporate Sister, *Dr. Jacque*

Acknowledgements

First, I would like to thank my Lord and savior Jesus Christ for all things that He has bestowed in and upon my life. While the good has been sweeter, the not-so-good has been instrumental in shaping my life lessons and this book. Next, I'd like to thank my husband, Patrick Colbert, for his patience, and most of all for his undying love for me. You've been my rock, and I am so glad that God sent you my way. To my daughter, Raven; thank you for the one-minute hugs and giggles; they're forever branded in my mind and heart. To Nekebra Stephenson and Ladonna Black, you've definitely made bonus a thing of beauty. I would also be remiss if I didn't say thank you to the world's best mommy for your unwavering love and continual, fervent prayers that are rendered on my behalf each and every day. To my sister, Sharon Walters, you will always make me smile—I love you!

Thank you to my brothers, Roy, Mark, Richard, Lance, Anderson, and Julian. Your support, laughter, humility, and love keep me grounded and in tune. To my wonderful editor, Amy Root Clements, thank you is simply not enough. You went far beyond the call of duty in making sure my book matched my brand. Your keen eye, insights, and dedication to ensuring each and every word resonated with ease have made Corporate Sisterhood what it is today. You remind me of what it means to go beyond a work relationship to truly becoming my sister's keeper.

To my three "besties," Marie, Stephanie, and Valerie, you continue to illustrate how iron sharpens iron. Each of you helped to bring out the best in me and for that, I will always be indebted. To the sixteen women who were instrumental in my initial research, thank you. To my Delta Sigma Theta Sisters of 31 Primed for Perfection, if I dare regress on the bonds of sisterhood, I am reminded of the deep connection that we share. I am also grateful to all the wonderful men and women who have helped to guide, shape, and influence my life over my leadership career.

I would also like to thank my sisters-in-law, Amelia Walters, Doreen Walters, Carol Lee, Lynnette Florence, and Patricia Colbert. Your acceptance, friendship, and love are unmatched. To Ms. Antonia McClammy, who was instrumental in pushing me through the summer months by saying, "You've got a story and you need to tell it," thank you. Those simple, yet powerful words always resonate in my soul. To "the sisters" of my spiritual studies, you've elevated my spiritual journey, you lend support, and you allowed me to be authentically me: no judgement, no fear, no pressure; you're woo-woo! Thank you! Finally, to all the women and men of the world who will flip through the pages of this body of work, I want to thank you for trusting your instincts in reading and sharing this book and also for advancing the journey of Corporate Sisterhood.

To inquire about having Jacque Colbert speak
at your next event or meeting:

Please email
Jacquepcolbert@gmail.com or beinspiredjc@gmail.com

Connect with Jacque Colbert

Instagram- @drjacquecolbert

Twitter- @JacqueColbert

FaceBook- Dr. Jacque Colbert

Cover photograph of Jacque Colbert credited to
Ke'er Orr of Point and Click Photography.

Additional Photography provided by Syda Productions with Gino Santa Maria,
and Kurhan Javindy. Book cover, front and back, designed by David James.